Orpheus in the Park

poems by
Rose Solari

The Bunny and the Crocodile Press
Washington, DC

Cover design by Randy Stanard of DeWitt Designs

Author photo by Jimmy Patterson

Typography by Cynthia Comitz, *In Support, Inc.*

Printing by *Printing Press, Inc.*, in memory of George Klear

Acknowledgments

Grateful acknowledgment is made to the editors of the following publications, in which many of these poems first appeared: *Parnassus: Poetry in Review:* "My Mother's Elephants"; *Gargoyle:* "Abortion Elegy: What I Know About Her," and "Elegy for the Sleeping Girl"; *Minimus:* "In the Garden"; *WordWrights:* "Achilles on Shore," "Premature Elegy," "Elegy for the Five-Sided Box," "Diagonals and What Is Real: Adonis and Aphrodite," "The Creek, the Woods: Hermes and Aphrodite," and "Spring and What Comes After"; *Health Journeys* (website): "Persephone, Triumphant" and "Two Women"; *IOTA 10th Anniversary Poetry Series CD:* "Elegy for the Virgin." Acknowledgment is also due to Argonne House Press, publisher of the chapbook, *Selections from Myths & Elegies* (1999).

Many people have helped in the creation of this book. Special thanks go to Sunil Freeman, Andrew Harvey, and Reuben Jackson, for being big brothers; Sara Levy, for sisterhood, *convertendis rebus adversis in res nitidas*; Grace Cavalieri, for being a ministering angel to poetry and poets, especially this one; Ron Baker, Miles Moore, and Richard Peabody, for their support at crucial times; and the staff of Alan Squire Enterprises, Inc., for generously making things happen.

The cover painting, *Mystic River,* is by Travis Hall, and is reprinted with permission of Travis Hall Studios and McLarry Fine Art. More of Mr. Hall's work can be seen at at *www.travishallstudios.com* and *www.mclarryfineart.com.*

For Jimmy Patterson and Cindy Matsakis

Contents

IV The Rose-Tree Garden

I

In the Script of the Gods

Achilles on Shore

Tougher than hands that have carried heavy ropes
all day in the summer sun is the heart that feeds
on itself, incapable of solace in the outer air. Harder
than most will be the man who knows that in only
one place is he weak, and who allows his lover
to see that, once, and by accident. On deck, he feels
the serious world surround him, knows the water
that rocks his dreams is the water that carries him out
beyond the reach of her voice or her heavy heart.
Inside the silence of other men, inside his armor,

he is most free. Hear what the world will say of him
later, his muscles carved into marble, his words
on the city's walls. Hear how the women will dream
of making him soften, like butter for baking. She
could have told them a few real stories, spoken
of the price she paid for igniting more than desire.
She knows more than he does of this particular kind
of war, of how the map we make can betray us,
turn us another way. Tonight in his bed made of skins
taken from other warriors, tonight in her silk, she sees

their farewells written tight in the script of the gods.
Mortal women cannot compete; the legends are full
of those who tried and lost more than their lives.
Turned into trees, or stones, or animals, they call out
at night to each other, remembering love like fruit
gone to rot in the damp island air. *Tell me a story*, she says,
but he is near-empty of words. However full his heart,
he will never be able to loose its weight in language.
He will hurt her tonight, she knows, and then say
he is sorry. Tomorrow, the boats pull out again—

there is always another war—and when he returns,
if he returns, he will be somebody else anyway.
They say she should be grateful for whatever it is

she has got. For him, loving and killing are part
of a single song, the one he sings to himself to lull them
both to sleep. He will blame her later for listening,
and for remembering. For now, he presses her head
against his chest, feels the tears he does not cry slip down
her face. She puts her ear to his heart and listens.
How the beat of the world grinds through his weary blood.

Hephaestus and Hera

How could she abandon the boy who only asked
that she protect him from his father? How could
the mother throw up her hands, cast out
the child she'd made to help her in her loneliness—
for already her husband wanders, ignores
the plaintive tone of her voice, turns the sounds
that not so long ago had won his heart
against her as he heads for the door. She covers
her swollen eyes with layers of makeup. And now

she looks at the boy she might have loved
and sees only herself, what she has become—pathetic,
miserable, a devoted wife turned to tricks beneath
any courtesan. For what is a child, after all,
but a string that attaches mother to father? How could she
believe she could make something perfect
all of her own? In the dark she leads him outside,
walks, holding his hand, to the edge of the cliff,
fakes one step as if into the air, and then, when

he follows, lets go of his hand. As she returns
to her room, she covers her ears from his cries. And he
uncoils his body from the crumple of his fall, touches
his injured foot, and stares up at the place from which
his mother's face still fades between the stars.
There are losses we cannot allow ourselves to know.
For now, he begins to work a fallen branch into the shape
of a splint for his foot. Then he changes his mind,
and begins to make something called art.

My Mother's Piano

What it must have cost her to carry that thing from rented apartment to rented apartment to rented house to the house they bought with the help of my father's GI bill to the house I grew up in—souvenir of her family's brief, mysterious period of prosperity, like my aunt's diamond ring, my mother's Wurlitzer baby grand. Big as a boat. Glossy as patent-leather shoes. A literal-minded child, I worried that it, like other babies I had seen, was going to grow, and grow a lot, eventually squeezing us out of the living room, so that we'd spend most of our time in the cold, damp basement, or trapped in the narrow upstairs hall. If there's a god, I used to think, why is my mother so sad and mean? Why is her memory so bad that she remembers the B I got in geography but not the long, long list of A's?

But I was talking about the piano—how she would smile when she sat down to it, closing her eyes as if the music that rose from her hands had hands of its own that massaged her face. How her fingernails would click against the keys, a backbeat I thought was so impossibly adult, like face-powder or the bright red polish she'd said I wasn't ready for yet. "Three keys past an octave," she would boast, stretching her fingers out to show me the span of her hands, and I'd put my girl-palm up against hers to measure the difference.

Okay, I think sometimes, so she could have been a teacher, a singer, even an actress; okay, I tell myself, she got a raw deal. She was still able, in the grace of the absence of words, to make something beautiful and good, her hands moving like light, like water over those keys. What came from her fingers then was a story, slow at first, and a little dark, speaking of generations who never had enough, and then of their children, and then of the fantasies that those children's children had—a curving staircase to walk down slowly, like Grace Kelly in a wide skirt, good light, smooth men with real jobs, real money, who knew their way with a cigarette lighter. Day to day my mother and I would be just two women who didn't know how not to hurt each other. But when she played, there was truce, always—her at her bench, me curled up on the rug beneath my mother's piano, both of us caught in the knowledge of all she'd never be.

Persephone, Triumphant

Six months up and six months down and she
is not afraid of anything anymore—not afraid
of him, of his hot skin, of how desire
falls from his back as he lifts up off
of her, satisfied and spent, for he always
comes back, and not afraid of her mother,
whose insistent grief had seemed at times
a huge mouth ready to swallow her alive.
She is alive and happy. She knows the underworld
and no one now can tell her stories, make her
hide beneath her bed. As a child, she jumped
at everything, prepared for invasions
of every sort, her mother blind in the way
that mothers have to be, it seems, to get by.
Now that's all over. Now the ones who laughed
at her innocence ask for instruction, count
on her kindness. Everywhere she is needed
somehow she appears—transcendent, light—
buffed by her suffering until she gleams,
taught by the darkness to be so bright.

In the Garden

1.

He lies sleeping beneath the branches
of a tree whose roots stretch down past imagining.
The light across his face plays gold,
then silver. In his upcurled hands,
the breezes spin their pollen like little worlds.
He belongs here. Everything belongs to him.

Yesterday, they made love in daylight
for the first time. She pushed her hair
out of her face so she could watch him.
At first he liked it—at first he seemed
to like new things—but after a while
he used his hands to cover her eyes.
She pushed them off. Now he dreams
a perfect mirror, perhaps a lake shaped
like the shadow of his body, as she

kneels beside him, ready to wake him up.
In the space between her slowly falling hand
and his left shoulder stars are forming. The shape
of something ripe hangs in the air. In the moment
before her fingers come to rest against his skin,
he will wake and blink and ask her what she wants.

2.

It must have been summer, everything swelling,
everything calling to them, dangling
from the trees, swaying deliberately, in the way
that says, *devour me soon, I will not last
for long.* It must have been late summer,
the lusciousness two steps away from death

that made her think, made her imagine
what might become of them after this.
For how long could they last, content
in each other's arms, nothing to do but love
and love some more, nothing to build or learn?

It must have been nighttime, her body lit
by the moon and stars. For days she had been
preoccupied, even unkind. He went for walks.
He took more naps. He thought, *forget about it.*
And woke to find her staring at the sky.
Sometimes, she said, *the world is so large and sweet
that I think I could eat it. Do you know what I mean?*

He almost knew. He thought
he knew. He did not want to know.

3.

Now we can bring the serpent into this
but I see her doing it alone—perhaps he displays
himself, his lovely body coiled along a branch
of the appropriate tree, but doesn't say anything.
She doesn't need him. He is just there,
the beautiful, beguiling object—scales like malachite,
onyx, amber, those stones we call only semi-precious—
and perhaps, for encouragement or distraction,
she even strokes him. Can you see her, one hand
still on this world, for a moment, the other caressing
the white keys of the piano, then finding
the black? Knowledge comes to us
through our desires. We take the beautiful
for our own and a world opens up.

He slides out of his skin.
She uses it to tie back her hair.

4.

For him, it had been enough—the world
small and graspable, the worn path he walked
every day, the stable, graceful, dependable shape
of her taking that same path, or curled against him,
napping, or floating across his dreams. Having her,
he had so much more than he'd thought possible after
those early days alone. The color of her hair
his favorite color. Her eyes the model for his own.

It was enough. It was more than enough. It was
contentment and the promise that it would last.

5.

Back at the tree, her open mouth, back
at the moment where everything spins—
as in a Hitchcock movie, we see images of the past
swirling around her, and melodramatic music
rising in waves. In the center, our heroine
sees none of this. She is engaged in the act
of breaking open the flesh of what feels
like one ordinary apple, her teeth delighting
in the last resistance—food is one
of her favorite things—and in the juice
that begins to fill her mouth. If we could
step in, would we tell her what we know?

They will be together always. They are
sentenced in that, anyway.

Elegy for the Five-Sided Box

It was only four months—the whole
of one long winter—that he stayed with me.
I thought to make his body the place I'd store
myself. On mornings so cold and dark
that neither of us could rise at the clock's
first ring, we lingered, holding each other
beneath warm pockets of sheets. Or I
held him. I don't know what he thought
he'd wrapped his arms around. And I

don't know when I began to gather
his fallen hairs into the five-sided paper box
another lover had used to give me a pair
of dangling rhinestone earrings, many years
in the past. I found the first strand
on the pillow, saved it as a whim. And then
there were others—trapped on the sink's ledge,
caught between pages of a book, snagged
on the doorframe, hooked on the edge

of a stereo speaker. Everywhere, the corners
of my house offered up the idea of him—
red-brown, longer than I'd imagined, straight
as a line. Trying to fit them into that box
became a game, became my work. Hair
doesn't fold, sticks to the fingers, won't stay
in place. I would pack the fine strands in tight
and close the lid, only to see them spidering out.
I tried tying them into knots to keep them

gathered and in place, I weighed them down,
after a while, with little stones. When I
was a girl, my mother kept, tucked
in the corner of her jewelry box, a brooch
her mother had given her, made of silver
and fine, black, ropy stuff I'd never seen

in any jewelry store. When I asked her
what it was, she said, *a mourning pin,*
made from some dead person's hair.

It frightened me, even then, to imagine
a woman—and more, a woman of my family—
sitting for hours braiding the hair
of her lost friend or spouse or lover
into the shape that lay on thin, fake velvet.
A double, interlocking oval. Almost
a heart. I never saw my mother wear it
and when she died, I did not ask where
it had gone. When he was gone, lost

to the warmer weather, with only words
for reasons, and not much of them, I found
myself one morning crouched beside the bed,
scanning the carpet for more hairs. I guess
you could say I scared myself. So I put an end
to what he'd been to me by burning, in a small,
cast-iron pot, the box of hair. The box burned quickly,
its painted pattern—either arrows or strands
of wheat, I was never sure—dissolved in flames

so blue their innocence hurt. His pain
a five-sided story he told himself to stay warm
at night. My body the vehicle that carried him,
for a time, back into himself. Hair smells
awful when it burns, as if complaining
of the indignity of flame that rises, hopeless,
that sings its own pure song regardless
of whatever it is it swallows. I pulled
a strand from my own head and burned that, too.

Abortion Elegy:
What I Know About Her

There are times I can see her face as if
she were here, as if she had lived—hair darker
than yours or mine, your cheeks, my mouth.
She stands over my bed as she did almost
a full year before we knew of her, or runs
through the living room, both hands spread,
chasing a shadow.
                I don't talk about this
to anyone, although I want to, want to be able
to say aloud when she would have been born,
how old she'd be right now, and how much
I would have loved her. If blood were fire,
she and I might have burned through circumstance,
might have been waiting, pure and calm,
whenever you came to us.
                      I imagine
too much, I know. It gives me rough dreams.
But sometimes, when it is very quiet, I know
I hear her. I ask her forgiveness one more time.
I explain, as if from the beginning, how we decided
she could not be, that there was no room for her,
and believe she understands. And returns
out of love, not vengeance, to where she started.

Elegy for the Sleeping Girl

Perhaps I make too much of it. Maybe my sister
has even forgotten that New Year's Eve when
the man she wanted to marry stood her up. Maybe
it's only me who still recalls the blue silk dress,
so tight my father turned his head away, and the hair,
a tall pile of sculpted curls. She'd dressed for
a big night, dinner and dancing and hints he'd dropped
that, tucked in the pocket of his dress uniform,
he'd carry the ring she thought would make her
whole. Twelve years older, she'd always been
a chaotic mystery to me, and that night I studied her
again, watching her brush the peach-colored powder
over her cheeks, spray herself with Windsong.

At 8:30, my father began to wonder aloud about
the traffic. At nine, she called the base; the corporal
on duty said he had, indeed, checked out. Then
my mother insisted on dealing her into a game
of rummy, but I played my sister's hand
while she paced, her body jerked to the window
by every sound—a car door slammed, our next-door
neighbors greeting guests. At 10:30, my mother hissed
that, Marine or no Marine, she'd give him a piece
of her mind. My sister already knew, of course,
that we'd never see him again. She went to bed,

slept until my mother woke her for the next night's
dinner. At the table, in her pajamas, her face bare
and pale, she looked to me like an ailing child, save
for her magnificent hair, tilted now a little to one side.
We didn't mention him. Her pain had made a space
around her no one, not even my mother, would dare
to enter. Maybe my sister has forgotten that man,
those hours, her life so busy now that memory has

no room to post its flags of humiliation. Accused,
always, in our family of making too much of things,
I might, in this case, agree except for this: years later,
she would name her first child after him.

II

Glass Emptied and Refilled

As If to Remind Us of Everything

we'd lost, the summer returned, for three
        sweet days, in fall. Too restless
to keep myself indoors, I wandered

the neighborhood, saw the outdoor tables
        full of couples in love. Already,
the old story had begun again—trees showing

the sky how many colors they'd kept hidden
        beneath their green, then shaking them
off, like memories or bad ideas. Outside

the Safeway, the skateboard boys took on
        the banisters, half-flights of steps
to the street. One, hair bleached near-white,

had a bracelet of thorns tattooed around
        his arm. Each time he landed, his body
rippled from feet to neck, and was

the more beautiful, being subject
        to the laws of ordinary matter. Further
down the block, I passed the store

you managed, the year we married. Only
        then did I remember it was
your birthday. I came home and opened

a bottle, raised a glass to you, and one
        to your new love. Then I made
dinner—small purple eggplants, tomatoes

swirled in golden oil. Garlic and parsley.
       Glass emptied and refilled. I know
we are happier now without each other, but

remember what it felt like when
       we weren't. The two sometimes
are hard to keep in balance. I think

of that boy pushing off of the ground,
       the concentrated grace that filled
his eyes; I think of the space between

his feet and board at the apex
       of his flight, charged with magic
all the more precious because it can't last.

Diagonals and What Is Real:
Adonis and Aphrodite

1. Proposal and Argument

They sit on the rocks and talk, this time,
about right and wrong, or about his mother,
as he constructs yet another argument against
the merging of their bodies. She wonders why
it should take so many words to refute a simple need—
if you don't want to, just say no—but he goes on
talking as if to himself, as if to the stars
who will weave their predictable magic
no matter what he says. Or does. Or doesn't.

And meanwhile, in her eyes, his already perfect
image glitters, grows, becomes so radiant
she forgets what she planned to say: that truth
requires detachment, a coolness no real lover,
so immersed in heat and light, can ever have;
that in love, two opposing concepts can be true,
as in, *we are so alike, we are nothing alike;*
that words are not the body, can only approximate,
can never reproduce, are not alive; that talking
not only can't prevent, but can never replace the act.

2. Watching Him

He moves across the landscape spread below
as if propelled by wind or wheels. Where
do his feet touch down? Does he walk
on the earth at all? He swings up
onto the steepest rocks as if his long and serious body
were no more than air. Sometimes she dreams
he is flying over her. Sometimes she dreams
she is on her knees, covered by his shadow.

So what begins in envy moves to adoration—
for how can she help but love the only human
who makes her feel insufficient, how can she help
but pursue the only one who takes pride
in his refusal? Not that his heart is pledged
to another—she could work with that—but that
he has other things on his mind than love or her.

3. What She Tells Herself

In her lucid moments, fewer and fewer now, she makes
the promise all breaking and broken-hearted lovers
make to themselves—*I'll just give it one more
month, one week, one hour, this is the last time*—
and is proud of herself for making it through
an afternoon without him. *This is the last time,*
she says, in yet another letter, *that I will write you,*
sealing and sending it or not, then tying her hair
and skirt in the manner he likes best. And repeats
to herself, *the last time,* as she follows him
into the woods, lies down beside him, strokes his face
in sleep and trembles all over again, as if
for the first time, at the translucence of the body
that houses his soul—how close to the surface floats
his heartbeat, how warm the blood that runs so near
beneath his skin—and which is more beautiful
and how the two compete, and prays, *this is,*
this must be the last time, pulling him into
her arms to wake him, weak on purpose, believing
the ground must surely shake itself into flower
beneath their bodies, so rich is the juice
that pours from him, so sweet his touch, however
cruel his words, so rapturous her assault that goes on
and on as if and always for the last time.

4. Him Alone

At night, he likes to run along the shore
on the rocks by himself. If it is cloudy,
if he cannot see where his feet will fall
beneath him, if he has to go by memory and by
the varying temperatures of stones beneath his
bare feet, he is most happy. He has never fallen,
nor given it a moment's thought.

He has never loved her.

For a while, he thought he did. He thought the heat
that filled her body indicated a reciprocal heat in him,
and so when she said, *Lie down. I know you want to,*
he did, and did again. And believed what happened—
the fierce outpouring of every impulse he had ever had
to kill or own or take, tempered now and then
by tenderness—was love. But now, by himself

beneath the moon, he admits that he can take or leave her.
That despite whatever his friends may say about all
he is giving up, it is the same if she comes or doesn't come,
tonight or any night. In fact, the skills he has uncovered
make him wonder what it would be like to try this game
again with others. At first, with just about any other.
And then, particularly with one or two.

5. How It Should End

Whether it ends with him spending half the year
with Persephone in the underworld and half with her—
a ridiculous tradeoff, how can we believe she'd go

for that?—or if he dies, killed by another
of her lovers, she never has a chance to get over him.
It is important to this version that she get over him.

So let's tell it this way: One day, as she is about
to go out and look for him again, sending another
lover off with a distracted kiss—can you imagine
the lovely camaraderie that his presence would create
among her suitors, how they'd unite against his youth
and transient prettiness, able to drink together,
share stories of his cowardice and her folly,
resting in each others' worth while they waited
to become enemies again?—she looks in the mirror
and hesitates. Laughs. Shakes her head and goes outside.

The air is very cool—it has gone from summer to fall—
and as she walks she lets down her skirt, unrolls
her sleeves, and undoes her hair. The sun is dropping
so that it almost meets her eyes, so that it hurts.
And she feels the memory of him fall from her body
like a dress she used to like to wear, a dress
she used to think said everything about her, but now
is silly. Boring. A little overdone. She walks until
her clothes are damp, until it is all, all gone. And then
she passes him. And smiles. And keeps going.

Ariadne's Lesson

Chances are, I think, she would have helped him
        anyway—daughter of a terrorized people,
whose lives were caught and twisted in fate's corkscrews,

and he the warrior, demon killer, son of a god.
        The wedding bargain was his idea, struck
in the giddy moment that precedes success. *If we*

defeat the Minotaur, we marry. Who knows how much
        either of them believed it could be done? It must
have seemed, from either side, like a good match—

her craft, his courage—but she sacrificed from the first
        her deepest mystery, and he had ship, sex, blood,
and homeland on his side. Once her beloved city

is out of sight, he begins to see two pictures of his future:
        in the first, Ariadne forever with him—beautiful,
yes, but strange, not of his own kind; in the other, he,

the solitary hero returned to glory, his choice of women
        spread out before him like stars in the night sky.
An intelligent girl, she knows before he does

which he'll choose, is dressed and ready when the soldiers,
        those dumb animals, come to lead her from
the ship. To be cast off, she tells herself, is to begin

again. On an island between gods, she reviews
        stories of the past. One might be of the girl she was,
longing, in all holy ignorance, for fate's test. One

might be of how he claimed her, despite her father. And finally,
        there's the tale of what she'd said: *I can help you—*
it is a phrase women like to use—*I am a girl who knows*

secrets, I'll give you one unbreaking strand to navigate
    the maze, and then your heart. She will know better
when the next boy-god arrives, waving his courage

like the flag of new country made for two. *I am no one,*
    she will say, *I have nothing to give.* And he, flattered
by such emptiness, will not be able to resist.

Persephone, Again

The first time it happened, I thought I must have imagined it—me with my boss in his office, discussing some routine thing not worth remembering, and then his hand up my skirt and his mouth squashed flat into mine. I was sixteen. It felt like he was trying to swallow my face.

My brother picked up my paycheck for me the next day and I never went back. School was about to start, anyway. But a few years later it happened again, this time with a boy I liked, one I wanted to date. My first year in college. The middle of the night. We were sitting on the concrete lip of a fountain, somewhere downtown, our friends lost or forgotten. A little drunk and giggling. I was waiting for him to kiss me.

Instead he came at me—not in the clumsy way I'd come to recognize of a boy who is, in fact, a little bit afraid of you, and so tries to hide it by diving in, like a kid afraid of the water—but hard and mean, as if he was angry at me for something. I remember how the concrete scraped my back as he held me down with one hand, unzipped his pants with the other. That time getting away was harder. That time I had to see him in some of my classes, hear my girlfriends say that he said I was a dick-tease.

After a while, I thought I knew how to stay away from the ones who will do it. After a while, I found out I wasn't the only one. But just a few days ago, at a lecture on classical mythology, I heard the speaker say that when Persephone was abducted by the god of the underworld—when she was pulled down against her will into the darkness she had never before encountered— this was something that needed to happen. "We need both halves to be complete," the speaker said. "Becoming an adult means having knowledge of both the lightness and the dark."

And I thought, *No.* I thought, *There are other ways to go from girl to woman.* No one would choose the path she had to take— Hades rising up out of the ground and into her body, the way that boy, possessed, I admit, by something he did not understand, had tried to carry his awful fire into me. If Persephone did not fight, I'm sure it was because she froze, as I did, gone cold and blank in the midst of all that heat and neediness.

The world outside of reason spins on no axis. A woman might spend her whole life searching for a stream that flows untainted by its poison.

Two Women

There are days she wants
to live, days she's ready to die.
Perhaps in that way, eighty
with emphysema isn't so different
from heart-sore and unemployed

at thirty-two. Either woman
might wake one morning to decide
that it's just not worth it; either might
be stabbed by joy large enough
to render pain, at least for a time,

invisible. Time is a bird the older
clasps in fingers broad at the tips,
holds onto like the memory of
her first full-length party dress;
time is a field the younger has,

right now, no heart to cross. What
they can't say to each other might ease
the elder's panic, salve the younger's
will. But love buckles between them,
twisted so that the flow is blocked—

as in a muscle, cramped, then starved
for air. The younger one wants
to give up; the older fights. How
funny, they both think. It should be
the other way around. In hospital rooms,

silence becomes the language we
all speak, machines filling the air with
clicks and beeps where heartbeat and song
should be. The older one had a beautiful
voice and a sure way with the piano

when she was younger; the younger one
has smaller hands, can't carry a tune,
as they say, to save her life. But
inside each is a song whose melodies
are near identical, in whose notes—

though the younger does not know it
yet—there is the signature for survival.

Spring and What Comes After

Somewhere behind this still-white hill
there is a woman waking up, turning over.
Quiet—can you hear her? Your hand
is not yet ready to reach toward hers,
her hair still falls across her eyes
which you are as yet unprepared to meet.
So it is just as well that she hesitates,
warming her wide soft body beneath
the beginnings of the sun. It is just as well
that she waits until the last snow has melted,
until her skin and yours have turned
a deep true brown, that she'll take her time.

III

Chambers of Light and Dark

Letter to My Father

Still beautiful, and still the first best place
I could ever call home, your eyes at the end
were not opaque, but simply elsewhere.
It took me a while to realize this wasn't
personal, that trying to call you back
with anecdotes or books wasn't wrong
but silly, like me as a child trying
to flag down planes that passed over our back yard
by waving my hands. You were more than ready—
you'd been preparing yourself for years
so that when whatever it was you saw
in those last days walked into the room,
your body would shed its names like water
to fit its indifferent arms. Now my body
feels as empty as yours must be—organs removed,
blood extracted, and the breath that carried
your soul in words to me now vanished in air.
Outside, birds sing their usual songs, water
slides or trips or runs, inexplicably the world
without you goes on. I could carry you
everywhere, like a stone in my shoe, and still
never see your face on this earth again.

After the Cliff:
Psyche Begins Her Story

Falling was the easy part. Once I decided
to trade my body for a breath, I had only
to close my eyes, let the broad, sweet back
of the wind carry me wherever it wanted.
Like pollen, I could glide though I could not
fly. Back on the cliff, my parents' bodies,
outlined against the gold-red sky, looked small
and strange, as if we were already made
of different elements. Then the unthinkable—
what felt like another body surfacing, as if
through water, beneath my own. *This is death,*
I thought at first, and was not scared, only
grateful to the gods for letting me pass
into the heavens on the back of this bright angel
and without pain. But the winged body beneath me
curved down, not up, and soon we were under
the clouds again, heading into a valley
I knew but did not know, as if I'd been there
in my dreams.

               I was my parents' golden girl.
The gods have saved the best for last, they said.
In you we have the fruit of all our sufferings.
I am not boasting—it is easy to be good. People wear
their stories on their faces, and what they want
is to hear their tales told back, but better. For them,
I played the loving daughter, the innocent girl,
the flirt, the brash young thing, the sullied flower,
the lie. They were all so happy. I cannot describe
my loneliness. Sometimes, at night, I would dream
of a golden boy—his mother's prayer, his father's envy—
someone like me, who had played many parts.
He would come as if I'd called for him, and the night
would fold around us a cape of stars, each one

sharp-pointed, ready to cut the masks away.
And in each other's arms there'd be no more stories.
All narratives, I thought, end with love.

                             And so
that evening, when he set me down on marble steps
that led to a house more lovely than any
I had seen, and fed me what I wanted, knew
my fatigue and when to take me up to bed,
and told me, after that first and precious night, that
it might be like this forever, so long as I never asked
to see his face, but was content to know him only
by his voice and touch and deeds, it seemed to me
not payment but reward. In this new world,
with only animals for company, and a creek
that sang my name and something else, I might
be free to be myself. I took this as an end.
It was the beginning of another story.

Cupid's Predicament

Say the world, by some bright accident, offers
you everything except what you most desire; say
the time is never right, that waiting will not
bring you closer to your goal; say your parents
deny the need, insist that you should love
what you are told, align your passions
to the world's efficient forms; say your will,
so innocent in itself, is bent, unblossomed.

Now see the impossible girl, the one wrong
choice, the form your mother cannot bear.
See how she bends to you, half-budded, green
at the stem. Sometimes the self, to preserve
itself, must store its nature in another.
Why not select the right companion, build
a temple, house yourself in it, in her.

Elegy for the Dark:
Psyche's Letter to Cupid

Even now, I think I should never
have insisted on bringing your body
into the light. I might still be lying
in my bed, hearing your footsteps round
my window, soft as a light wind
rounding the leaves, waiting to catch
the glint of your eyes like remembered stars
in the blue-black night. I did not need
to hold that too-bright lamp to know
you, to feel how the length of your body
was filmed with soft, curling hair—
like fur, like fire—or to know
your scent, that of a creature caught
in the transformation from animal to man.
You liked what I liked—fingers taken
between the lips, and words that move past
speech to cries, and silence afterward, when
the beating heart recovers its lost
image. It was like prayer, the way we
touched each other. I'd pray to you now,
if I believed it would bring you back
into my bed. At first, when you didn't
return, I thought, *Oh, give it time, he
cannot stay away, he will forgive.*
After all, I only asked for the sight
to adore you fully, oh, my precious angel
of winter night. Tonight, when the rain
began, I believed for a moment that what
I heard was the brush of your fingers
against my window, and I rose—can you
imagine? For such are the unbroken habits
of love—to look in the mirror, make
myself beautiful for the one who does not
want to look, who will never come again.

Cupid's Disappearance

Call it reflex. Call it the self-preserving
act of the newly freed, already threatened
with another set of chains. With her
in the dark, he could allow himself
any tenderness. Light embarrassed him,
and so light made him cruel. But if you think
she had the worst of it, think again. For she
could walk out in the world with her soul
in her eyes, bleed her suffering into the ground,
into action, wear the truth of her love
like skin. But he feels the double sorrow
of having lost and having no mirror
in which to see it. Now, having given up
the knock at the window, traded the open
mouth of desire for the closed twin doors
of duty and what is right, he cannot enter
anymore the room he'd made, the image
and the echo of himself. Pain that cannot
see itself cannot be eased. And so he makes
of his grief his armor, beneath which
the heart, desperate for an answer, longs
to be either comforted or broken.

Psyche Remembers Where She Started

In my heart, I do not know how I could have
done other than what I did. They came to me
with their flaming eyes, their lips pressed close
together to keep the hunger in, and said, *Help me
live.* No, that is not right. They said, *Give me life.*
And if you, in your innocence, describe to me
how you would have walked past them, told
yourself it was not your fault the sun was rough
against their skin and the infinite night was so
unkind, spreading its black wings over
their houses, beating down hope, blotting out
light, while you and yours were graced with gold
and ripening olives—well, I would say
that you know little, then, of the power
of others' suffering. Their pain was real—
it was not invented to make me fling myself
from the edge of a rock too steep for any body
to survive the fall intact, much less alive.
If you'd seen famine, you'd know its ravages
cannot be feigned. Yes, they were cruel.
Need strips us naked, peels from each
petitioning soul its cushioning kindness.
But they believed that by my sacrifice
I could save them, and their belief became
mine too. With my body, I built the bridge
between their suffering and their desire,
pulled them with me, for a moment, into
hope's wide and bottomless arc. They did not
really want me dead, they wanted death,
and then rebirth into something better—
as hard to come by as a clean, untattered
moth's wing pressed to the cheek, as difficult
to number as love or blood. When
was the last time you pressed your knees
to the ground for anything? They knelt and asked
for everything I had. I gave it to them.

The Creek, the Woods:
Hermes and Aphrodite

1. How It Began

At first it was words, all words.
He could say how much he wanted her
in so many different ways. But language
was his medium—the clear lit grotto
through which he passed from one world
to the next—so while she loved
to hear him talk that did not woo her.

Then he took her sandal.

He stood at the rim of that bright creek—
My creek, she thought, *my world, my light*—
and dangled it by its straps above the water.
Not saying a word. And she crossed over
to his side slowly, picking her way
among the stones, giving him time
to see exactly what he had coming—
born out of the sea of her father's sperm,
what would she look like?—and lay down
before him.

                    What are you
offering me? he asked, and she said, *More.*

2. Her Thoughts

He was a talker. Unlike her husband,
he was thinking all the time. But in their union,
something dissolves—you're like an orchid,
she told him once, you open up for me
in the night and then you're gone.

For he might fall on his knees, beg her
to always love him, and the next day leave
for another country. At first, it scared her.
Then she got used to it. Then she liked it.

Being immortal, they didn't worry
about running out of time.

Each one thinks sometimes of the lessons
of Narcissus and wonders if the other is only
a mirror, the self shot back in snatches
from the jeweled mesh of the water.
You could lose yourself in the sweetness
of your own image and never get out.
But if that's it, how to explain
the consistent and unweakening response.
I want you all the time, he tells her. *And I, you.*

At first, it was all body. Then the body
became everything that was.

3. What He Wants to Know

I come to you because you're the expert,
he said. *Is this love?* That was beside the creek,
afterwards. The first time. She didn't answer.
When he came back, sleepless, embarrassed,
already hard, he said, *Is this love?*
She laughed and pushed him off the path,
into some bushes. Away from her for weeks,
negotiating, making deals, he would lie down
at night, his chest tight with the thought
of the two of them wrapped around each other,
and think, *Is this feeling love?*

Meanwhile, sitting under the sun drinking wine
with some young boy, assuring him that of course
she'll help him win the girl he loves,
while all the while her fingers linger
gently on his thigh, she watches his face
go bright, then pale, she thinks
this one is almost too easy, and he,
well, he is forgetting about the girl—then
she remembers, somehow, her lover, thinks
of his hipbones fitting precisely between
her own, and of the rose-colored flush that rises
from her fingertips to her throat when he walks
beside her, when he looks down into the river
of her body before he enters, dipping a finger in,
then lifting it to his mouth, she hears his breathing
and his question, and she thinks, *Yes.*

4. Why He Took Her Sandal

Because his life in all its busyness
had become a little predictable.
Because he'd been trying to seduce her
for so long it didn't matter whether
the method worked or not—it was just
a pastime, a way to keep his hand in,
as it were. Because the sheer luscious vanity
of the object made him want it for its own sake.

Because it smelled like her. Because he wanted
something but didn't know what it was.
Because he knew she wanted to give in,
but after all this time would need
a new good reason. Because she'd had it on
when they first met. Because she loved it.
Because he knew it would make her laugh.

Because he wanted to see her angry, wanted
to see what she would do to counter him.
Because taking her dress would have been
too obvious. Because her feet were lovely,
narrow at the heels, with thin straight toes.
Because he hoped she'd let him put it on
again—winding the laces around her ankle,
around her calf, to where the muscle swells
then dips to the back of her knee, where he
could kneel, he thinks, forever,
all bewilderment, delight.

When you're not with me, how do I know
you exist at all?

5. How It Goes On

Sometimes she hears the complicated machinery
of his mind running on, running without her,
running into the cold plain yellow light
that brings the end of summer. Sometimes the fierceness
of his arms around her wakes her in the night.

Now they are awake. He stands behind her,
looking through her hair at the trees now bleeding
gold and red and orange, and feels the wind move
through his body, blurring his edges with the soft clay
of her skin, blurring his eyes to green rainwater.
She leans back. Sometimes he loves her whole
unmitigated weight; sometimes he'd have her
heavier, or lighter. But since the first assent,
neither one has thought of saying no.
She laughs at the trails he leaves. They are
just enough alike, and they are lovers.

Deer

You said she looked like a beautiful naked
woman, coming out of the trees, wary
but not frightened, ready to counter
any move we made toward her. We moved
toward each other, your hand probing the tear
in my jeans as if you were searching for something
precious—fifty-year-old single-malt scotch,
maybe, or a silver, five-pointed star. At first,
I could not stop watching her while, almost sure
of us, she lowered her head to the grass. Then
there was nothing but your hair and the curve
of your neck beneath it, the sound of our breath
and that other, wilder whisper, the breeze
coming up from the valley, tender on our skin.
The next day, hiking without you far off
the road, I spotted a buck climbing the hill.
When he saw me, he stood stone-still and met
my eyes. And I thought how hard each of them
must work to be worthy of the other, and how
neither one, neither one, has to say a word.

Morning Invocation, Taos

for Ebby Malmgren

Earlier than the first before first morning light
I've learned to wake, walking the chamber inside
the chamber that will unfold into waiting day.
See how the light comes across these walls, not
in fingers or poured honey, but as itself, particle
and wave, moment and time. I step outside, where
nothing can come between me and sky, between
the gravel caught in my boot and the cloud that
carries rain to the valley two valleys from mine.
Yes, to these mountains. Yes, to this life I leave
and pick up, leave and pick up. I ask the dawn,
not for blessing, but only to come, and come again,
in gusts of hummingbirds, handfuls of earth spread
on the air, circles of monarch wings, and a spilling yard
of sunflowers, balancing on thick stems the weight
of their heavy heads in the turning world.

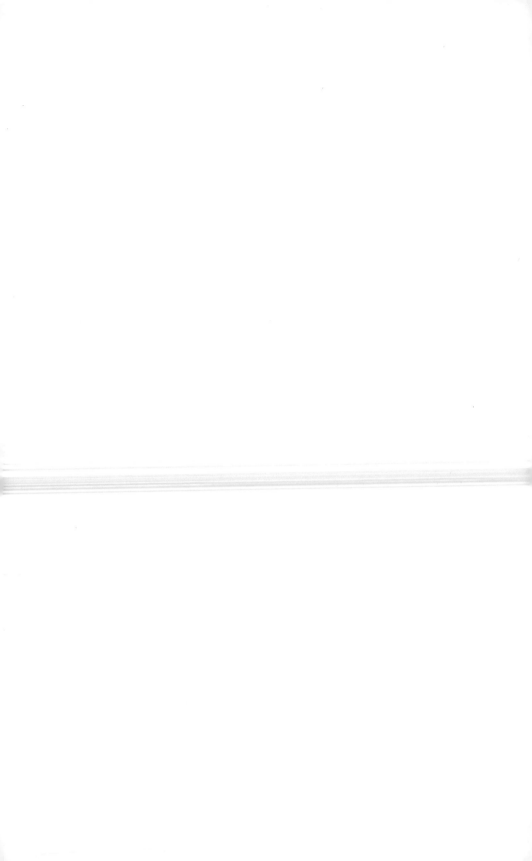

IV

The Rose-Tree Garden

Orpheus in the Park

For all the time he can remember
it has been his—a voice that hits,
secure, the center of each note,

as in the often heard but no less worthy
image, the arrow that carves in two the one
before that split the one before that hit

the target's flag-red, heart-red center. If
you heard him, as you walked, maybe,
through a city park in spring, saw his feet

beat out the time while he strummed and sang,
turning the golden lyric into dark earth,
then into gold again, you might have wept.

> *It's only a story*, your companion says,
> for comfort. It's the only story
> this boy will ever tell.

The gods are jealous, and know us
to be weakest and most worth envy when
in love. So when the girl, near-but-never-to-be

a bride, walks in the grass, she does not see
the glittering, ignorant thing that will make her tale
worth singing. As fangs sink into skin, she begins

to cry out, then thinks, *how silly. I will die,
anyway*. Her body falls. The soul penetrates
the ground, mist after rain.

> Science says wherever we walk, we change
> the future. Myth says every step we take
> is a step into the past.

What if her loveliness, that is, her human body,
was like a dress—the thing she used to cover
her real self—and being longed for only

shrank her in her skin. *They love me
for my flesh, which is not me.* So, when
the snake strikes, rising fast for the narrow ankle,

it gives her respite she may not have known
she wanted. How quick, the move that lifts us
out of time and into the never-again.

There is love that rises, and there is love
that falls. How could he know which kind
his song would be about?

No matter how the music hurts, it hurts less
than life. As you sit weeping at some concert,
perhaps, your lover at your side, you feel

the luxury of created hurt, a worked echo
of the spinning blades slung by your own desires.
Later, safe in your bed, you think, *I was not*

myself. I was not in my right mind. Still,
you long to hear it one more time, the tune
only half-unfolded, half-light, half-gone. A girl

who wants to be air. A boy who is song. What
is this life, then, but a means to get to the other side,
where voice and body, being one, no longer fight.

Persephone, Knowing

Hungry for it, yes, and wouldn't you be,
her whole short life given to wandering
the fields of her mother's will. Everything
made to keep her safe, designed for the child
she was told to be. No wonder she wanted
to break through the close arms of mother-love,
the fertile land that told her just and only
what she was good for. And so she began again
in the underworld, stitched a new self from
the cloth of her husband's loneliness, discovered
her gifts for untangling and deciding. Here,
there were mortal pleas that were hers

to answer. A boy hunting with song for his dead bride;
a woman ready to trade her life for a box that holds
infinite beauty; a warrior searching for comrades,
finding his mother. These were her people—the maimed,
the brooding, the lonely, the desperate. She listened,
loving the tellers for their honesty, how they, like her,
risked all known worlds for the one beneath their feet.
Her visits to the place of her birth were like leaving
the soul for the body. Inhaling the too-moist scent
of land turned for planting, her mother's welcoming
embrace, she would long already for her dry home,
where death was everywhere, and knowable, and sweet.

Elegy for the Virgin

When, at seven, I watched him rising,
shirtless, from the blue corrugated circle
of his parents' Sears Roebuck pool,
saw him run the bright towel, imprinted
with football players helmeted and leaping,
over his arms and legs, then shake
his hair from side to side, the water
spinning for him a halo of falling light,
I ran to my older sister's room, to tell her
the ultimate thing had happened: I had fallen
in love. The boy next door, no less—his mother
grew roses, red and pink, and had given him

her gray eyes. It leads here, I thought,
years later, lying beneath that first lover, all
the fumbling and fear, it was for this. How soon
did I realize that every time I touched someone,
another possibility blinked out. And the radiance
we found was not the kind that surges through
the body playing kickball or jumping rope
summer nights, but more like the beam
of a flashlight you carry into the cellar
again, when you can't sleep. You almost know
what you're doing. You can almost see what
you're trying to find. Sometimes, I try

to imagine my body back to its virginity.
Did I know something in my untouched state
lost to me now so long, I've forgotten its shape?
Sometimes, I wish I could live again, for a week,
for a month, in a world not cracked by feeling, not
made dangerous by desire, where it was
blessing enough, and all I wanted on this earth, to see
Brian Fugel, eleven years old, in his chopped,

low-rider Levi's, standing in the apple-less Eden
of his mother's rose-tree garden, a bearer
of mystery, but no despair.

Premature Elegy

Dearest, in those moments when your breath falls
like warm powder on my cheek, when you are falling
away from me into the sweet exhaustion of your sleep,
sometimes I feel, I think, a premonition of what
your death will be. I watch you fading like the candle
we let burn to the very bottom of its holder, and then
beyond, the wax running over the surface of the mantle
while we—do you remember?—rolled from couch
to rug to floor. You said I roared in your ear that night
like a tiger. You said I pulled you into me, then burst
right through you. Oh, love, while I am lying by
your side, watching you enter into dreams I cannot
follow, I feel the bigger loss of you already circling—
your voice still living in small, sharp echoes in my ears,
while I lie here, kissing the air above me into the shape of you.

Achilles Grieves: Two Songs

Into this life, one friend who reveals the self—

     The gates swing shut, then open.

say what you will of it, no one could

     A song of all potential tumbles out.

move him closer to himself than he

     Life's design will be made known

who makes this journey now to the other side,

     to the one who seeks it, singing

offerings packed in his hands. Achilles finds

     the praises of the gods, his fate

the boat late and lingers, remembering.

     in their hands. Powerful is the story

Once the beloved is gone, he will leave behind

     of how we meet our destiny; strong

all mortal longing and attachment, he'll relinquish

     is the voice we tell it in, full of

love, as they had known and fought it,

     our own bright beauty. We can be close

the double embrace of muscle and skin, the songs

     to the gods in this—our acquiescence

at firelight, the comfort of met desires.

     to whatever the fates have made us,

He steps on board, believes the spirit

     what we've been asked for, what we

of his dead lover feels it, sings

     bartered in return. Ah, glory. Celestial.

the rhymes back now, to soothe the echoing

     Purified of longing. Place of rest. Happy

of his abandoned heart. The gods ask too much.

     the man who dances lightly toward the end

Before he follows, he will make sure

     of his own story. Happy the people

they know what he thinks of them.

     who can retell these tales of glory.

My Mother's Elephants

Because of their size, and the shape of their ears,
and the sweetness and wisdom she claimed to see
in their miraculously-lashed eyes, my mother,
for as long as I can remember, loved elephants.
At the zoo, she would linger, chuckling, before
their house, the babies in particular seeming to hold
some charm for her, their wrinkled legs belying
their years. Someone in cruelty had called her
an elephant once when she was a girl because of her size,
which she could not control, despite a diet of not much
more than cigarettes and over-perked coffee. Perhaps
her fondness for those creatures started then,
a way of turning the pain around, as after her death
I would tell my friends that it was easier to love
my mother now that she'd lost the burden of her body.

When she began to collect them—china, brass, and seashell,
carved into the tops of wooden or pewter boxes, blown
out of glass—it was a relief to all of us, I think, to have
something to give this woman who almost no gift could please.
Now she had found one small, true thing that could never
fail her. Regardless of value, she adored them all, arrayed
them across the piano, her dresser, the windowsills,
as if, like guard dogs, they marked the perimeters of her turf.
She hardly went out at all by then. The cough that embarrassed
her children, rising as it would at all the worst moments,
kept her at home. And then the oxygen, of course, those last
years of hers attached to a metal tank. Long after the dusting
and polishing had become an impossible chore, we still
brought them to her like flowers, like a language
without anger that we had found, at last, to speak.

The weekend after my mother's funeral I drove
to the beach, thinking I might uncover, at the meeting
of sand and water, better words than the priest
who mispronounced her name had used to say goodbye.

It was May and raining, though each morning of those three days
I put on my bathing suit, and wore it beneath my clothes
as if desire alone could change the weather. On the last night,
with no answers yet to whisper into the emptiness you feel
when your best enemy has fallen to infinite silence,
I went for one more walk on shore, and threw into the waves
the last present I'd given my mother—a small, silver elephant,
its trunk raised up like a greeting, like a promise of something
better, not only rest and peace but please, I prayed, some
happiness for that woman whose heart, so bruised by time
and sorrow, might yet, in another life, be healed by joy.

Elegy for My Twenties

It is a different kind of happiness from being
loved but I maintain that it is still happiness,
the small euphoria that comes of being

alone and accountable to no one. Sundays,
especially—I'd lie in bed late, shaky from
too much wine or something I shouldn't have

done the night before. Then it was time to roam
the neighborhood, high on coffee and ready
for something to happen. Something usually did,

even if only a sudden, particular slant of light
that washed the streets for a moment
pale rose, pale gold, or a blush and a grin

from the teenaged boy at the video counter,
like I was something sweet he could almost
taste. I'd buy myself chocolate, eat it slowly

while the sun did its falling-down dance between
oaks and elms. Surrounded by stroller-pushers,
sometimes I thought I was the only single person

in that town. And I loved it. Oh, I know I was often
lonely—I had nightmares and was afraid, a lot
of the time, in fact I was terrified—but in memory

in my twenties I am an amazon of solitude, a goddess
of standing firm on your own two feet. That girl
is brave and hungry, a little fatigued, maybe, but full

of her own wild self. Her jeans fit well. Her hangovers
fit well. She rocks. She glows. I never tire
of looking back at that comic-book heroine,

watching her scale the slick glass sides of buildings labeled school, career, confidence, sex. I think she's a wonder. I can't wait to see what she'll do next.

Poem for Grace

for Grace Cavalieri

When it comes, if it comes, it will come to us
not for the asking, but through the Lord's mercy,
which, from what the nuns said, was vast and yet
unpredictable. Like talent, I thought, or good skin:
some have it, and some of us don't. If it falls,
it will fall like roses tumbled from the sky,
as they did from the robes of Saint Teresa,
another story inside a story, another lesson
we had to learn without knowing why.
Then I preferred the tale of Saul, knocked blind
from his horse by God's brilliant desire to save
his soul, raised up as Saint Paul, lucky
to be stricken, proof of the light that could
shatter us whole. But now that I'm older,
I know I would rather be struck by grace,
which comes when it comes by quiet accident,
sun in the midst of a long-stormed winter,
or rain on crisped grass. And when we turn
upward to meet her blessing, what we need to be,
even more than grateful or humble, is ready,
worthy of all her complex gifts, and how
she unfolds for us, petal on petal, interleaving, aflame.

Beach With Oyster Stakes

After the painting, Oyster Stakes
by Helen Torr, 1930

All day my slack-slung chair pushed
down and back beneath my weight
into the sand. All day, I almost left.
Too salt, too mean, too much, this place—
and me, reduced, shifting inside
an old windbreaker, sunk in myself
like an earring dropped and vanishing
into the dunes.

        Still, the clouds keep
shifting their mighty shoulders; still,
the blue-gray water laps in almost
predictable rhyme. Two flags, slapped
by the wind, mark oyster beds, drunk
on their isolation, almost outside
of time.

        It can take a long time
to love what you're given; it might take
all you have not to ask for more. The waves
in their 2/4 time won't ignore my weakness
or clap for my luck. I'm lucky to have them,
anyway, ready to sing into oblivion
whatever it is I came here to give up.

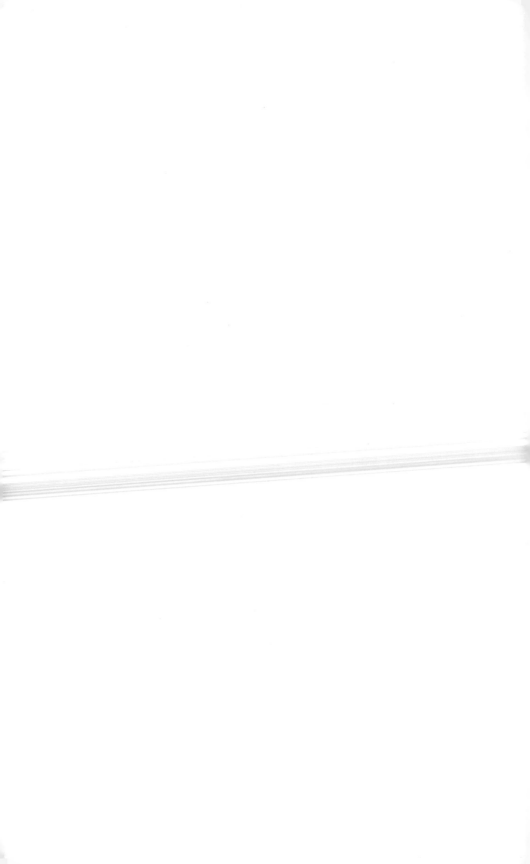

Lovers, Warriors, Children:
A note on the myths behind the poems

The book you hold in your hands is made up of two intertwined strands of poems. One strand consists of elegies—poems of celebration and farewell, written for my late parents, as well as in honor of relationships, ideas, and illusions that have passed on. The other is made up of retellings of tales found in classical mythology.

When I first introduced some of the myth-based poems at live poetry readings, I discovered that many listeners were unfamiliar with the source stories, or had, over time, forgotten them. I began to give brief, extemporaneous summaries of the various stories and characters that had found their way into my work. Audiences seemed to appreciate the small doorways that these summaries opened into the poems, and so, when it came time to put the poems into book form, I thought it only made sense to accompany them with the same sort of background material.

What follows is a brief and admittedly personal, rather than scholarly, survey of the myths mentioned here. For easier reading, I've listed the central characters below in the order in which they first appear in the book, and they are italicized on first mention.

One of the most recognizable figures in the book is *Achilles*, Greek hero of the Trojan War. In *The Iliad*, Homer describes him as dazzlingly swift-footed on the battlefield, terrifying in his rage, and the greatest warrior not only of his own time, but of all time. There are other dimensions to Achilles, as well. He is tenderly protective of his beloved younger cousin, Patroclus, who is also a soldier, if not a very good one. When Achilles is insulted by his captain, Agamemnon, he refuses to continue fighting, and Agamemnon begins to fear that his greatest warrior is planning an insurrection. But Achilles without a war to win seems surprisingly content. Sent to coax him back into battle, Odysseus finds Achilles surrounded by his men, playing his lyre and singing to them of the adventures of great warriors past. His rage, it seems, can be tempered by art.

"Achilles on Shore" is set in a time shortly before the Trojan War. When I wrote it, I was thinking of the men in my family who have been to war—my father, my uncles, my brother—and of the women who loved, prayed for, and waited for them.

Further on in the book, I return to Achilles late in the war, just after Patroclus has been slain. Achilles' grief is all the greater because he is in some way responsible for that death. After Achilles refuses Odysseus' attempt to bring him back into battle, Patroclus makes a brave and foolish decision—he steals his cousin's uniquely made and very recognizable armor, and wears it into battle in order to fool the Trojans into thinking that Achilles is fighting again. Hector, Prince of Troy, kills Patroclus, believing him to be the Greek army's great warrior. Achilles' enormous, aching grief for Patroclus and his thirst for vengeance against Hector drive him back into battle.

"Achilles Grieves: Two Songs," is cast, as the title suggests, in two voices. The one on the left side of the page is that of a narrator who sings Achilles' private thoughts, including his anger at his captain and the gods themselves, and his love for his dead cousin. The italicized voice, which runs down the right side of the page, is a group voice, modeled on the choruses in Greek tragedy who speak in unison, interpreting the onstage action for the viewer. Here, the chorus gives the reader the public or official version, an interpretation of Achilles' last days that transforms individual grief into patriotic glory.

Achilles' armor, in particular his famous shield, was made by *Hephaestus*, god of craft and metalwork, whose creations are, Homer says, "a wonder to behold." Unlike most of the other gods, who range from physically perfect to dazzling, Hephaestus is as homely as his works are beautiful. He is also lame in one leg, victim of a boyhood injury.

The story of Hephaestus' wounding exists in various versions. His parents, Zeus and Hera, are king and queen of the Greek gods—they rule over Olympus, or the heavens, and can either bestow great blessings or inflict great pain in their dealings with mortals and other gods. They are also frequently at war with each other over Zeus' constant infidelities. In one version of Hephaestus' story, Hera manages to impregnate herself with him, hoping to regain her husband's attentions with the mystery child. When Zeus remains indifferent, she throws the boy off of Olympus. In another version, Hephaestus intervenes in one of his parents' many quarrels, and Zeus, infuriated, throws the boy to earth. At the time I wrote the poem, "Hephaestus and Hera," there had been a sequence of deeply disturbing stories in the national media about women who had killed their children. It was Hera I was thinking of as perpetrator when I came to write about this tale of a discarded child.

Persephone, on the other hand, is a much-loved child, daughter of the nurturing goddess of the harvest, Demeter. Hades, god of the underworld, kidnaps the girl, taking her underground to live as his queen and preside with him over the souls of the dead. Demeter, in her grief, neglects her work and soon the earth becomes a kind of reflection of her suffering—the crops wither, the ground is dry and barren, and the people starve. Zeus intervenes and strikes a bargain between husband and mother. For six months of each year, spring and summer, Persephone will live with her mother on the earth; fall and winter, she will reside with her dark husband in the underworld.

This is one of those wonderful myths that give narrative meaning to natural phenomena. It is also one whose layers of meaning continue to pull me back to it. It's a story about mothers and daughters, about daughters and husbands. It's a story about leaving home. It's a story about light and dark, about this world and the underworld. It's a story about one way that a child might become an adult. And there is still so much more, here, to explore. There are three poems for Persephone in this book, and I have reason to believe that she is not done with me quite yet.

The story of *Adam and Eve* was, I think, the first myth to take root in my own life, and was certainly among the most frequently retold tales of my Catholic girlhood. On the surface, it's a simple story. In Genesis, the first book of the Bible, God creates "the heavens and the earth," the plants and animals, and finally Adam, the first man, who God assigns to rule over it all. God sees that Adam is lonely—while all the other living creatures have mates, he is alone—and so, while the man is sleeping, God takes a rib from his side and makes from it a woman, a companion for him, Eve. The two reside for a brief and blissful time in the Garden of Eden, which, in illustrated Bibles, always seems to look a lot like Maui—palm trees, lush green foliage, sunny blue skies. Who, we might ask ourselves, would not be content there?

But as in so many myths, there is a condition to be met, a price for this happiness. God tells Adam and Eve that the Garden and everything in it is theirs to do with what they will, except for one stricture—they must not eat the fruit of the tree of knowledge of good and evil.

Satan, disguised as a serpent, persuades Eve to eat the fruit; she in turn convinces Adam to eat it as well. God knows of their disobedience immediately, and casts them out of Paradise and into the cruel weather of the human world. Now, we are told, they will have to work for their daily bread—a penalty that has far more significance to me now than when I was a child. But more than God's wrath or Satan's trickery, what I was interested in here was the relationship between the two human beings. I wanted to explore the marriage of Adam and Eve for patterns that also hold true in contemporary relationships, particularly one eternal conflict—the need for domestic tranquility and safety pitted against the desire for the unexplored, the forbidden, the new.

Some of my earliest retellings were poems on *Aphrodite,* the Greek goddess of love and beauty, known to the Romans as Venus. One is based on a story that always makes me smile, the tale of Aphrodite's unrequited passion for the beautiful mortal youth *Adonis.* He must be lovely, indeed, to snare this beautiful-above-all goddess—in his poem about them, Shakespeare devotes ten lines to Adonis' dimples alone. But the idea of romantic love leaves the boy unmoved. Adonis would much rather go boar hunting with his friends and sleep out under the sky than lie in Aphrodite's arms, and he is not shy about telling her so. Yet Aphrodite pursues him with greater and greater wildness, panting, cajoling, weeping, begging, even pretending once to fall down dead, slain by the unkind look in his eyes.

Part of the enduring human charm of Aphrodite is, for me, her willingness to make a fool of herself, a trait that I was unaccustomed to in a deity. The Judeo-Christian God may be a lot of things, but you're never tempted to laugh at him. But Aphrodite's pursuit of Adonis is, in its self-dramatizing excess, hilarious.

It also reminds us of a few uncomfortable truths. No matter how sophisticated we may want to seem, all of us, at one time or another, will make fools of ourselves for love. And no matter how clever, persuasive, or desirable we are, no one, not even the goddess of love herself, can have anyone they want. There will always be somebody resistant to our charms.

The second Aphrodite poem here is about her tryst with *Hermes,* the messenger god who could travel between worlds. I love the playfulness of the first encounter between these two veterans of the love-wars—the story has it that he steals her sandal while she's bathing, and she wins it back by making love to him.

Ariadne lives under the shadow of a family curse, and, like many an unhappy girl, she looks to love to rescue her from her troubled home. She is the daughter of Minos, King of Crete, who ascends his throne with the help of Poseidon, the god of the sea. Poseidon sends Minos an enormous bull that must be sacrificed to the god in gratitude for the help he has given the king. But Minos cannot bring himself to kill the magnificent animal, wanting instead to keep it for himself. As we have seen from other stories, the gods hate human ingratitude more than anything, and they have swift and awful ways of punishing it.

In this case, Poseidon makes Minos' wife, Pasiphaë, fall passionately in love with the bull. They mate, and she gives birth to a monstrous child, the Minotaur, who has a bull's head and a man's body, and who feeds on human flesh. Humiliated, Minos must pay and pay again for his ingratitude to Poseidon, and for his wife's resulting unnatural act. He has the great craftsman Daedalus conceal the Minotaur inside an impenetrable labyrinth. Minos also provides the creature with yearly human sacrifices, boys and girls taken from Athens and sent into the labyrinth to die. Though from time to time some brave soul tries to kill the Minotaur, no one ever succeeds, and no man is ever able to find his way out of the labyrinth alive.

The Athenian prince, *Theseus*, arrives pretending to be a sacrifice, but with a secret plan to kill the Minotaur. Theseus is crafty, ambitious, and, against all reason, supremely confident. Ariadne and he make a bargain. She gives him a thread to unspool behind him as he makes his way into the center of the labyrinth, where the Minotaur lives, as well as a sword to kill the beast. If he succeeds, he can find his way out by following the thread. He agrees that if her thread-plan brings success, he will take her back to Athens and marry her.

Theseus kills the Minotaur, and he and Ariadne set off on what the girl believes is her wedding voyage. But Theseus has second thoughts about keeping his side of the bargain. Instead of taking Ariadne home with him to Athens, he makes a detour, and deposits the young woman alone on the island of Naxos. We do not know how long she wandered there, how she fed herself, what she might have thought. But in some versions, her story has a happy ending—Dionysius, the god of wine, revelry, and ecstatic transformation, finds her on Naxos and falls in love with her. As with some other mortals in these stories, the gods reward her for her brave good faith and compensate her for her suffering by giving her the gift of immortality.

The tale of *Cupid and Psyche* is all about the cost of various kinds of love. Here, Aphrodite appears in her Roman guise as Venus. This time, the goddess of beauty is insane with jealousy over the mortal girl, Psyche, whose loveliness the people have begun to say rivals that of Venus herself. There is always a big price to pay, in these stories, for being compared to the gods. Venus decides to take revenge on the girl by sending her son, the mischievous boy-god of love, Cupid, on a mission with his famous bow and arrow. Even the gods fear this boy's weapon—hit by Cupid's arrow, the injured party falls in love with whomever or whatever she is looking at when pierced. Venus orders her son to shoot Psyche when the girl is looking at the most hideous man in her village. Upon seeing Psyche for the first time, Cupid, overwhelmed by her loveliness, makes a strange and beautiful choice—he deliberately shoots himself, choosing to fall in love with the girl.

Her first plan having failed her, Venus punishes Psyche's town with plague and famine. An oracle tells Psyche's parents that the city will only be saved if their beautiful daughter is sacrificed to the god of the mountain. Psyche says that she will go willingly in order to save her people. But when she leaps off the mountain into seemingly certain death, Cupid arrives to break her fall.

In the most well-known section of the tale, pieces of which survive in later stories such as "Cinderella" and "East of the Sun, West of the Moon," Cupid, afraid of his mother's wrath, installs Psyche in a palace tucked far away from other human company and visits her only at night, in the dark. The condition of their continuing love is that she cannot see his face. Like Eve in the Garden, Psyche chooses the risk of knowledge. She holds a lamp up to her sleeping beloved, and discovers that he is not, as she had feared, some kind of monster, but a beautiful young man. But her relief is short-lived. He wakes and, furious with her for breaking their pact, flees to his mother's house.

Venus then gives Psyche a series of four increasingly impossible-seeming tasks to perform in order to earn the right to see Cupid again. She must sort a huge pile of seeds and beans into their separate heaps in a single afternoon; she must gather golden wool from the fleece of sacred sheep known to kill all who come near them with their sharp horns and poisonous teeth; she must scale a treacherous glass mountain to fill a jar with water from the rushing river of death, the River Styx; and finally, she must travel into the underworld and ask Persephone, Queen of Hades, to give her a boxful of divine beauty to take back to Venus.

With help from various natural and supernatural entities, the girl completes the first three tasks, and most of the fourth. But she cannot resist taking a peek into the box before handing it over to Venus. When she lifts the lid, a cloud rises up out of the box, casting her into immediate, deep sleep. Psyche collapses, the box open beside her.

Something in that collapse seems to trigger Cupid's courage. He flies out of his mother's house and to his lover's side. He petitions the gods to support his choice of a beloved, and even Venus gives in. Cupid and Psyche are married with his mother's full approval, and for the girl's courage and persistence, she is granted immortality by the gods.

Finally, we come to *Orpheus*—the great poet, singer, and musician said to be able to charm both the gods and the wild beasts and make the rocks and trees move with his songs. Like Achilles, his power derives from being the best at what he does. He loves Eurydice, another famously beautiful girl, who is bitten by a snake and dies on their wedding day. Orpheus persuades the gods to let him enter the underworld and, with the power of his song, convinces Persephone to let him lead Eurydice back to the land of the living. Persephone gives him one condition: that he not look back to see if his bride is indeed following him until he is out of Hades. At the last instant, he forgets and turns around in time to see Eurydice fading back into the underworld. He loses her twice.

The poem I made in tribute to him, "Orpheus in the Park," contains, I think, some sense of the book as a whole. It was, in part, out of grief for my parents' deaths, three months apart, that I turned to the old stories, hoping that they might help me find meaning in, if not comfort for, my loss. But the longer I worked with the mythological material, the more I became convinced that any sense of separation between the two is artificial; there is, finally, no distinction between the extraordinary and the ordinary, between myth and everyday life. Rather, the two interpenetrate, infusing each other with meaning. In stories of Orpheus and Psyche, Hephaestus and Persephone, Achilles and Aphrodite, we find bits of ourselves, as well as others we have loved and despised, needed and feared, clung to and lost.

–Rose Solari
Bethesda, Maryland
January, 2005

Rose Solari has been the recipient of many honors and awards for her writing, including the Randall Jarrell Poetry Prize (selected by Philip Levine), an Academy of American Poets' University Prize, grants from the DC Commission on the Arts and Humanities and the Maryland State Arts Council, and an Exceptional Merit Media Award (EMMA), given by the National Women's Political Caucus and Radcliffe College for excellence in journalism. Her first full-length collection of poetry, *Difficult Weather*, was selected for the 1995 Columbia Book Award for poetry by Carolyn Forché. She also authored and performed in the multimedia play, *Looking for Guenevere*, which retells Arthurian legend from a woman's perspective. She is currently working on a historical novel.